The Child Who
Never Grew

D0862263

The Child Who Never Grew

A Memoir

PEARL S. BUCK

INTEGRATED MEDIA

NEW YORK

The Child Who Never Grew appeared as an article in *Ladies' Home Journal*, May 1950.

Cover design by Mauricio Díaz

978-1-5040-4796-8

This edition published in 2017 by Open Road Integrated Media, Inc.
180 Maiden Lane
New York, NY 10038
www.openroadmedia.com

The Child Who
Never Grew

I

I have been a long time making up my mind to write this story. It is a true one, and that makes it hard to tell. Several reasons have helped me to reach the point this morning, after an hour or so of walking through the winter woods, when I have finally resolved that the time has come for the story to be told. Some of the reasons are in the many letters which I have received over the years from parents with a child like mine. They write to ask me what to do. When I answer I can only tell them what I have done. They ask two things of me: first, what they shall do for their children; and, second, how shall they bear the sorrow of having such a child?

The first question I can answer, but the second is difficult indeed, for endurance of inescapable sorrow is something which has to be learned alone. And only to endure is not enough. Endurance can be a harsh and bitter root in one's life, bearing poisonous and gloomy fruit, destroying other lives. Endurance is only the beginning. There must be acceptance and the knowledge that sorrow fully accepted brings its own gifts. For there is an alchemy in sorrow. It can be transmuted into wisdom, which, if it does not bring joy, can yet bring happiness.

The final reason for setting down this story is that I want my child's life to be of use in her generation. She is one who has never grown mentally beyond her early childhood, therefore she is forever a child, although in years she is old enough now to have been married and to have children of her own— my grandchildren who will never be.

The first cry from my heart, when I knew that she would never be anything but a child, was the age-old cry that we all make before inevitable sorrow: "Why must this happen to me?" To this there could be no answer and there was none. When I knew at last that there could never be an answer, my own resolve shaped into the determination to make meaning out of the meaningless, and so provide the answer, though it was of my own making. I resolved that my child, whose natural gifts were obviously unusual, even though they were never to find expression, was not to be wasted. If she could not make the contribution she should have made to her generation through her genius for music, if her healthy body was never to bear fruit, if her strong energies were not to be creatively used, then the very facts of her condition, her existence as it was and is today, must be of use to human beings. In one way, if not the other, her life must count. To know that it was not wasted might assuage what could not be prevented or cured.

This resolve did not come to me immediately. I grew toward it, but once I had reached it I have held to it through all the years of her life. I have let it work in quiet ways, dreading the cold eyes of the curious. Now, today, I will forget those whom I dread, who, after all, are very few. I will remember the many who are kind, who will understand my purpose in telling this story, who will want to help to fulfill this purpose because it is their purpose too.

I am always moved, with grateful wonder, by the goodness of people. For the few who are prying or meanly critical, for the very few who rejoice in the grief of others, there are the thousands who are kind. I have come to believe that the natural human heart is good, and I have observed that this goodness is found in all varieties of people, and that it can and does prevail in spite of other corruptions. This human goodness alone provides hope enough for the world.

I have sometimes wondered, as the years passed, whether the moment would come when I might feel that my purpose for my child must include the telling of her story. I dreaded this, and do dread it. Nevertheless, the time has come. For there is afoot in our country a great new movement to help all children like her. It is too late, of course, for her to be helped, but it is not too late for many little ones, and surely for others yet to be born. For we are beginning to understand the importance and the significance of the mentally retarded person in our human society. Almost one person in every hundred is or will be mentally retarded, and of these the majority are retarded from non-inherited causes. The old stigma of "something in the family" is all too often unjust.

The total number of retarded children is not large in proportion to the whole population, and yet it is enough to cause trouble everywhere. Homes are unhappy, parents distraught, schoolrooms confused by the presence of these who for no fault of their own are as they are. As parents die or cannot care for them, as teachers give them up, these children drift helplessly into the world, creating havoc wherever they go. They become the tools of those more clever; they are the hopeless juvenile delinquents; they fall into criminal ways because they know not what they do. And all they do is done in innocence, for of God's many children these are the most innocent.

I rejoice in the dawn of a better understanding of such children, for the public attitude until now has been a sorely mistaken one. Parents have been bewildered and ashamed when their child is backward, when he cannot learn in school, when perhaps he cannot even learn to talk. It has been a misfortune to be hidden. Neighbors whisper that So-and-so's child is "not right." The family is taught to try to pretend that poor Harry or Susie is only slow. The shame of the parents infects all the children and sorrow spreads its blight. The child himself, poor little one, feels, though he cannot comprehend, his own inferiority. He lives in surrounding gloom. His mother cannot smile when she looks at him, and his father looks away at the sight of him. In spite of their tender love for him—for the honor of the human heart, it can passionately protect the helpless creature who is its cross—the child understands enough to know that there is something unfortunate about him. His shadow falls before him, wherever he goes.

Now, thank God, the shadow lifts. Wise men and women are beginning to reason that it is only common sense to accept the mentally retarded person as part of the human family, and to educate him in the things he can do, so that he may be happy in himself and useful to society. That this may be done, the primary work of research must progress as it never has. We must somehow discover why it is that so many people do not develop mentally to their full capacity. There must be remediable causes and certainly there are preventable causes. We know, for example, that if a woman has German measles in the first three months of pregnancy, her child may be born mentally defective, but we do not know why. We must know why. The Mongoloid child can appear in any family. He is really an unfinished child and is usually a first or last child. We must find out what conditions in the mother cause this child. It is not necessary that children be born never to grow to their fullest selves. The windows are opened, at last, upon this dark corner of human life and the light shines upon the children's faces and into the hearts of their parents.

That my child, therefore, may have some small share in creating this new light, I tell her story. She cannot know what she does, but I who am her mother will do it for her and in her name, that others like her may have the benefits of a fuller knowledge, a better understanding. It will not be easy to tell it all truthfully, but it is of no use to tell it otherwise. Perhaps when it is finished there will be comfort because it is told for a high purpose.

I must go back into the early years of my young womanhood—no, even before that. When I was a little girl myself, not more than seven years old, living in China, I had an awakening of the spirit. Until then I suppose I was the usual selfish childish creature, thinking of play and of nothing else except having my own way. I had few children to play with and one of my dear friends was a gay young American woman, who lived for a very short time next door to us. She was married, and during the few months she was our neighbor she had a baby girl born to her. It was my first experience of an American baby and of all the tender care that the average American baby gets.

Every morning I was the attendant at the bath. I poured the water and warmed the towel and handed the mother the little garments, one by one. I was allowed a moment of my own, when the fair-haired blue-eyed little baby, smelling sweetly of soap and freshness, was put into my arms. That was the height of the day for me. I can remember even now, even after I have held so many babies in my arms, babies of many colors and races, the joy of that first little one. I might have grieved very much when the transient neighbors went their way, had not my own little sister been born, fortunately, that same spring in the heart of the vast old city on the Yangtze River which was then my home. I busied myself mightily about our own baby. My mother was desperately ill after the birth, and the chief care of the baby fell upon our old Chinese amah and me. I was so happy I did not know how near my mother was to death.

I have begun this story so long ago because I can see now that I loved my child long before she was born. I wanted children of my own, as most women do, but I think my intense love of life added depth to natural longing. Something certainly I learned from the Chinese, who value children above all else in life. The Chinese love children for their own sakes and beyond. Children mean the continuity of human life, and human life is wonderful and precious. I absorbed the atmosphere in which I was reared.

My child was born in the height of my young womanhood. I was full of strength and vigor and the enjoyment of life. My life lay in places which might seem strange to my fellow

Americans but which were not strange to me. My home then was outside a small mud-walled town in North China. From my windows I looked over miles of flat farm land, green with wheat and sorghum in the summer, and in the winter the color of dust. Springtimes were loveliest, for above the young green wheat mirages shimmered. We had neither lakes nor mountains near, but the mirages brought them to us. They hung like fantastic dreams above the horizon. It was difficult to believe that they were not real.

Like every young woman, I had many dreams. There were books that I wanted to write when I had lived enough to know life. Life I had always wanted in plenty and overflowing, and I think, looking back, that I always ran to meet it. Certainly I always wanted children. So when I knew my first child was to be born, one year in the spring, my joy rose to the height of my dreams. I did not know then that there was to be only one. I did not think of such a possibility. Everything had always gone well with me, all my life. I was one of the fortunately born. I took good fortune for granted. I saw my house full of children.

I remember so well the first time my little girl and I saw each other. It was a warm mild morning in March. A Chinese friend had brought me a pot of budding plum blossoms the day before, and a spray of them had opened. That was the first thing I saw when I came out of the ether. The next thing was my baby's face. The young Chinese nurse had wrapped her in a pink blanket and she held her up for me to see. Mine was a pretty baby, unusually so. Her features were clear, her eyes even then, it seemed to me, wise and calm. She looked at me and I at her with mutual comprehension and I laughed.

I remember I said to the nurse, "Doesn't she look very wise for her age?" She was then less than an hour old.

"She does, indeed," the nurse declared. "And she is beautiful too. There is a special purpose for this child."

How often have I thought of those words! I thought of them proudly at first, as the child grew, always healthy, always good. I remember when she was two months old that an old friend saw her for the first time. The child had never seen a man with a black mustache before and she stared for a moment and then drew down her little mouth to weep, though some pride kept her from actual tears.

"Extraordinary," my friend said. "She knows already what is strange to her."

I remember when she was only a month older that she lay in her little basket upon the sun deck of a ship. I had taken her there for the morning air as we traveled. The people who promenaded upon the deck stopped often to look at her, and my pride grew as they spoke of her unusual beauty and of the intelligence of her deep blue eyes.

I do not know where or at what moment the growth of her intelligence stopped, nor to this day do we know why it did. There was nothing in my family to make me fear that my child might be one of those who do not grow. Indeed, I was fortunate in my own ancestry on both sides. My father's family was distinguished for achievement in languages and letters, and my mother's family was a cultivated one. On her father's side my child had a sturdy ancestry, which had occasionally produced persons of distinction. I had no fears of any sort—indeed, I was almost too innocent of fear. I had seen in my youth only one defective child, the little son of a missionary, and he had made no impression on me beyond one of love and pity. Of Chinese children of the sort I had seen none. There seem to be very few, and such as there are remain at home, carefully tended. Perhaps, too, they die young. At any rate, no young mother could have been less prepared than I for what was to come.

My little daughter's body continued its healthy progress. We had left North China by then, and were living in Nanking, which, next to Peking, perhaps, is China's richest city in history and humanity. Though my home was inside the city walls, it was still country living. Our house was surrounded by lawn and gardens, a bamboo grove and great trees. When the city walls were built, centuries ago, enough land was enclosed so that if the city were besieged, the people would not starve. Our compound was surrounded by farms and fish ponds.

It was a pleasant and healthy home for a child. She was still beautiful, as she would be to this day were the light of the mind behind her features. I think I was the last to perceive that something was wrong. She was my first child, and I had no close comparison to make with others. She was three years old when I first began to wonder.

For at three she did not yet talk. Now that my adopted babies have taught me so much, I realize that speech comes as naturally to the normal child as breathing. He does not need to be taught to talk—he talks as he grows. He hears words without knowing it and day by day increases the means of conveying his widening thoughts. Still, I became uneasy. In the midst of my pleasant surroundings, in all the fresh interest of a new period in Chinese history when the Nationalist government was setting itself up with such promise, I found life exciting and good. Yet I can remember my growing uneasiness about my child. She looked so well, her cheeks pink, her hair straight and blond, her eyes the clear blue of health. Why then did speech delay!

I remember asking friends about their children, and voicing my new anxiety about my child. Their replies were comforting, too comforting. They told me that children talked at different ages, that a child growing up in the house with other children learned more quickly than an only child. They spoke all the empty words of assurance that friends, meaning well, will use, and I believed them. Afterward, when I knew the whole tragic truth, I asked them if they had no knowledge then of what had befallen my child. I found that they did have, that they had guessed and surmised and that the older ones even knew, but that they shrank from telling me.

To this day I cannot understand their shrinking. For to me truth is so much dearer than any comforting falsehood, so much kinder in its clean-cutting edge than fencing and evasion, that the better a friend is the more he must use truth. There is value in the quick and necessary wound. Thus my child was nearly four years old before I discovered for myself that her mind had stopped growing. To all of us there comes the hour of awakening to sad truth. Sometimes the whole awakening comes at once and in a moment. To others, like myself, it came in parts slowly. I was reluctant and unbelieving until the last.

It began one summer at a seashore in China, where the waves come in gently even in time of storm. It had been a mild and pleasant summer, shore set against mountains. I spent the mornings with my child on the beach and in the afternoons sometimes we went riding along the valleys on the small gray donkeys which stood for hire at the edge of the beach.

The child had now begun to talk, only a little, but still enough to quiet my fears for the moment. It must be remembered that I was wholly inexperienced in such children. Now my eyes can find in any crowd the child like mine. I see him first of all and then I see the mother, trying to smile, trying to speak to the child gaily, her gaiety a screen to hide him from the others. But then I did not see even my own child as she really was, I read meaning into her gestures and into the few broken words. "She doesn't talk because she gets everything she wants without it," a friend complained. So I tried to teach my child to ask for a thing first. She seemed not to understand.

I must have been more anxious than I knew, however, for I remember I went one day to hear an American visiting pediatrician give a lecture on the preschool child, and as I listened to her I realized that something was very wrong indeed with my child. The doctor pointed out signs of danger which I had not understood. The slowness to walk, the slowness to talk, and then when the child could walk, the incessant restlessness which took the form of constant running hither and thither, were all danger signs. What I had taken to be the vitality of a splendid body I saw now might be the superenergy of a mind that had not kept control of the body.

After the meeting was over, I remember, I asked the doctor to come and see my child. She promised to come the next day. I told no one of my growing fear and through that sleepless night I went over and over in my mind all the good signs, the things the child could do: that she could feed herself; that she could put on her clothes, though not fasten buttons; that she liked to look at picture books; that she understood so much more than she could say. But I did not want false comfort. I wanted now and quickly the whole truth.

The doctor came the next day and sat a long time watching my child, and then she shook her head. "Something is wrong," she said, "I do not know what it is. You must have a consultation of doctors. Let them tell you, if they know."

She pointed out to me the danger signs I had not seen, or would not see. The child's span of attention was very short indeed, far shorter than it should have been at her age. Much of her fleet light running had no purpose—it was merely motion. Her eyes, so pure in their blue, were blank when one gazed into their depths. They did not hold or respond. They were changeless. Something was very wrong.

I thanked her and she went away. Thinking it over, I saw there was no reason why a stranger should stay to tell me more. Perhaps she knew no more. There is no task more difficult than to tell a parent that the beloved child will never grow to be an adult. I have done it sometimes since, and I have not allowed myself to shrink from it, but it has been hard. The heart can break more than once.

The doctors met the next day. I can still see the scene as though it took place before my eyes now. The house had a wide veranda, facing the sea. It was a glorious morning, and the sea was violet blue and calm except for the gentle white surf at the coast. The child had been with her Chinese nurse playing on the sand and wading in the water. I called and they came up the path between the bamboos. In spite of my terror, I was proud of my child as she stood before the doctors.

She had on a little white swimming suit and her firm sun-browned body was strong and beautiful. In one hand she held her pail and shovel and in the other a white shell.

"She looks well enough," one of the doctors murmured.

Then they began to ask questions. I answered them with all the honesty I had. Nothing but honesty would do now. As they listened they watched and they began to see. The shell dropped from her hand and she did not pick it up. Her head drooped. The oldest doctor, who had known my parents, lifted her to his knee and began to test her reflexes. They were weak—almost nonexistent.

The doctors were kind men and I begged them to tell me what they thought and then tell me what to do. I think they were honest in their wish to do this. But they did not know what was wrong or, whatever was wrong, how to cure it. I sat in silence and watched the child. I began to feel that they were agreed that development had stopped in the child, but they did not know why. There were so few physical symptoms—only the ones I have mentioned. They plied me with questions about the child's past, about her illnesses: had she ever had a high temperature, had she ever had a fall? There had been nothing. She had been sound from her birth and so cared for that she had never been hurt.

"You must take her to America," they told me at last. "There the doctors may know what is wrong. We can only say there is something wrong."

Then began that long journey which parents of such children know so well. I have talked with many of them since and it is always the same. Driven by the conviction that there must be someone who can cure, we take our children over the surface of the whole earth, seeking the one who can heal. We spend all the money we have and we borrow until there is no one else to lend. We go to doctors good and bad, to anyone, for only a wisp of hope. We are gouged by unscrupulous men who make money from our terror, but now and again we meet those saints who, seeing the terror and guessing the empty purse, will take nothing for their advice, since they cannot heal.

So I came and went, too, over the surface of the earth, gradually losing hope and yet never quite losing it, for no doctor said firmly that the child could never be healed. There were always the last hesitant words, "I don't want to say it is hopeless"; and so I kept hoping, in the way parents have.

It was getting harder all the time for another reason. The child was older and bigger and her broken speech and babyish ways were conspicuous. I had no sense of shame for myself. I had grown up among the Chinese, who take any human infirmity for what it is. Blind people, the lame, the halt, the tongue-tied, the deformed—during my life in China I had seen that all came and went among others and were accepted for themselves. Their infirmities were not ignored. Sometimes they were even made the cause of nicknames.

For example, Little Cripple was a playmate of my own early childhood, a boy with a twisted leg. According to our western notions, it would have been cruel to call him by his deformity. But the Chinese did not mean it so. That was the way he was, literally, and his twisted leg was part of himself. There was some sort of catharsis even for the boy in this taking for granted an affliction. Somehow it was easier than the careful ignoring of my American friends. The sufferer did not feel any need to hide himself. There he was, as he was, and everybody knew him. It was better than any sweet pretending that he was like everybody else.

More than this, the Chinese believed that since Heaven ordains, it was a person's fate to be whatever he was, and it was neither his fault nor his family's. They believed, too, with a sort of human tenderness, that if a person were handicapped in one way, there were compensations, also provided by Heaven. Thus a blind person was always treated with respect and even sometimes with fear, for it was thought he had a perception far beyond mere seeing.

All the years my child and I had lived among the Chinese we had breathed this frank atmosphere. My Chinese friends discussed my child with me easily as they discussed their own. But they were not experienced enough to know what was wrong or even that it was wrong. "The eyes of her wisdom are not yet opened," was the way they put it. "For some persons wisdom comes early and for others late—be patient."

This was what they told me. When we walked on the narrow winding streets of our old city no one noticed when she stopped reasonlessly to clap her hands or if, without reason, she began to dance. Yes, the Chinese were kind to my child and to me. If they did notice her, it was only to smile at what they took to be her pleasure, and they laughed with her.

It was on the streets of Shanghai that I first learned that people were not all so kind. Two young American women walked along the street, newcomers from my own country, I suppose, by their smart garments. They stared at my child and when we had passed one of them said to the other, "The kid is nuts." It was the first time I had ever heard the slang phrase and I did not know what it meant. I had to ask someone before I knew. Truth can be put into brutal words. From that day I began to shield my child.

There is no use in giving the details of the long, sorrowful journey. We crossed the sea and we went everywhere, to child clinics, to gland specialists, to psychologists. I know now that it was all no use. There was no hope from the first—there never had been any. I do not blame those men and women for not telling me so—not altogether. I suppose some of them knew, but perhaps they didn't. At any rate, the end of each conference was to send us on to someone else, perhaps a thousand miles away.

One famous gland specialist gave me considerable hope, and we undertook a year-long treatment with dosages of gland medicine. It did my child no good, and yet I do not regret it, for from what I learned that year I was able to save another child who really needed the treatment a few years later. I saw a little boy who at four was still crawling on his hands and knees and I recognized in his symptoms—the dry skin and hair, the pallid flesh, the big ungainly weak body, the retarded mind—the need for thyroid treatment. I did not know his mother very well, but remembering the silence of my friends, I went to her and told her what I thought. There was a long moment when her flushed face showed me her inner struggle. She did not want to know—and yet she knew she must know. I went away, but afterward she did take the child to the gland specialist and he was able to help the boy become normal. That boy was not really mentally retarded. He was suffering from a thyroid deficiency. Years later the mother and I met on different soil and she thanked me for that past day. But it took courage to speak. It always does.

The end of the journey for my child and me came one winter's day in Rochester, Minnesota. We had been sent finally to the Mayo Clinic, and day after day we had spent in the endless and meticulous detail of complete examination. My confidence had grown as the process went on. Surely so much study, so much knowledge, would tell me the truth and what to do with it.

We went at last into the office of the head of the children's department. It was evening and almost everybody had gone home. The big building was silent and empty. Outside the window I saw only darkness. My little girl was very tired and I remember she leaned her head against me and began to cry silently, and I took her upon my lap and held her close while I listened. The doctor was kind and good. I can see him still, a tall, rather young man, his eyes gentle and his manner slow as though he did not want anyone to be hurried or anxious. He held in his hand the reports sent in from all the departments where my child had been examined, and he made his diagnosis. Much of it was good. All the physical parts were excellent. My child had been born with a fine body.

There were other things good too. She had certain remarkable abilities, especially in music. There were signs of an unusual personality struggling against some sort of handicap. But—the mind was severely retarded.

I asked the question that I asked now every day of my life: "Why?"

He shook his head. "I don't know. Somewhere along the way, before birth or after, growth stopped."

He did not hurry me, and I sat on, still holding the child. Any parent who has been through such an hour knows that monstrous ache of the heart which becomes physical and permeates muscle and bone.

"Is it hopeless?" I asked him.

Kind man, he could not bear to say that it was. Perhaps he was not really sure. At least he would not say he was sure. "I think I would not give up trying," was what he finally said.

That was all. He was anxious to get home and there was no more reason to stay. He had done all he could. So again my child and I went out of the doctor's office and walked down the wide empty hall. The day was over and I had to think what to do next.

Now came the moment for which I shall be grateful as long as I live. I suppose to be told that my child could be well would have meant a gratitude still higher; but that being impossible, I have to thank a man who came quietly out of an empty room as I passed. He was a small, inconspicuous person, spectacled, a German by looks and accent. I had seen him in the head doctor's office once or twice. He had, in fact, brought in the sheaf of reports and then had gone away without speaking. I had seen him but without attention, although now I recognized him.

He came out almost stealthily and beckoned to me to follow him into the empty room. I went in, half bewildered, my child clinging to my hand. He began to speak quickly in his broken English, his voice almost harsh, his eyes sternly upon mine.

"Did he tell you the child might be cured?" he demanded.

"He—he didn't say she could not," I stammered.

"Listen to what I tell you!" he commanded. "I tell you, madame, the child can never be normal. Do not deceive yourself. You will wear out your life and beggar your family unless you give up hope and face the truth. She will never be well—do you hear me? I know—I have seen these children. Americans are all too soft. I am not soft. It is better to be hard, so that you can know what to do. This child will be a burden on you all your life. Get ready to bear that burden. She will never be able to speak properly. She will never be able to read or write, she will never be more than about four years old, at best. Prepare yourself, madame! Above all, do not let her absorb you. Find a place where she can be happy and leave her there and live your own life. I tell you the truth for your own sake."

I can remember these words exactly as he spoke them. I suppose the shock photographed them upon my memory. I remember, too, exactly how he looked, a little man, shorter than I, his face pale, a small, clipped black mustache, under which his lips were grim. He looked cruel, but I know he was not. I know now that he suffered while he spoke. He believed in the truth.

I don't know what I said or even if I said anything. I remember walking down the endless hall again alone with the child. I cannot describe my feelings. Anyone who has been through such moments will know, and those who have not cannot know, whatever words I might use. Perhaps the best way to put it is that I felt as though I were bleeding inwardly and desperately. The child, glad to be free, began capering and dancing, and when she saw my face twisted with weeping, she laughed.

It was all a long time ago and yet it will never be over as long as I live. That hour is with me still.

I did not stop trying, of course, in spite of what the little German had said, but I think I knew in my heart from that moment on that he was right and that there was no hope. I was able to accept the final verdict when it came because I had already accepted it before, though unconsciously, and I took my child home again to China. I shall forever be grateful to him, whose name I do not even know. He cut the wound deep, but it was clean and quick. I was brought at once face to face with the inevitable.

II

What I am writing is no unique experience. It is one common to many parents. Every retarded child means a stricken, heartsick family. I meet often nowadays with parents' organizations, parents of mentally deficient children who are coming together in their deep need for mutual comfort and support. Most of them are young people, and how my heart aches for them! I know every step of their road to Calvary.

"The schools won't take our children," one of them said to me the other day. "The neighbors don't want them around. The other children are mean to them. What shall we do? Where can we go? Our child is still a human being. He is still an American citizen. He has some rights, hasn't he? So have we, haven't we? It's not a crime to have a child like ours."

No, it is not a crime, but people—teachers in schools,

neighbors—can behave as though it were. You who have had a mentally deficient child know all that I mean.

When the inevitable knowledge was forced upon me that my child would never be as other children are, I found myself with two problems, both, it seemed to me, intolerable. The first was the question of her future. How does one safeguard a child who may live to be physically very old and will always be helpless? Her life would in all likelihood outlast my own. We come of long-lived stock, and though I might live to be old myself, I was borne down by grief and fear and she had no burdens on her happy, childish mind. Worry and anxiety would never touch her. What if she lived to be even older than I? Who would care for her then? Yet there was a strange comfort in her happiness. As I watched her at play, myself so sorrowful, it came to me that this child would pass through life as the angels live in Heaven. The difficulties of existence would never be hers. She would not know that she was different from other children. The joys and irresponsibilities of childhood would be hers forever. My task was only to guarantee her safety, food and shelter—and kindness.

Yes, I have learned as the years passed to be intensely grateful for the fact that my child has no knowledge of herself. If it had to be that she could not be a fully developed human being, then I am glad she has remained a real child. The pitiful ones are those who know dimly that they are not as others are. I have seen them, too, and have heard them say humbly, "I know I'm dumb," or, "I know I'm nuts," or "I can't never git married because I'm queer." They do not fully understand even what they say, poor children, but they know enough to suffer.

Thank God my child has not been one of these! She has been able to enjoy sunshine and rain, she loves to skate and ride a tricycle, she finds pleasure in dolls and toy dishes and a sand pile. She likes to run on a beach and play in the waves. Above all is her never-failing joy in music. She finds her calm and resource in listening, hour after hour, to her records. The gift that is hidden in her shows itself in the still ecstasy with which she listens to the great symphonies, her lips smiling, her eyes gazing off into what distance I do not know.

She has her preferences for certain kinds of music. Church music, especially hymns, make her weep, and she cannot listen to them. I know how she feels. There is something infinitely pathetic in that chorus of wavering human voices raised to the God in Whom, not seeing, they must needs trust. She dislikes intensely all crooning and cheap rhythms, and in general popular music of all sorts. If someone puts on a jazz record, she seems in an agony. "No, no," she will say, "I don't like it." It must be taken not only from the phonograph, but away out of the room. But she will listen to all the great old music with endless delight. When she was at home this last summer she heard Beethoven's Fifth Symphony through entirely, sitting motionless beside the instrument. When it was finished she wanted it all over again. Her taste is unerring. By some instinct, too, she knows each one of her own large collection of records. I do not know how, since she cannot read, but she can distinguish each record from the others and will search until she finds the one that suits her mood.

I put this down because it is one of the compensations, and parents of other children like her ought to know that there are such compensations. These little children find their joys. I know one little boy—I say "little," and yet he is a grown man in body—who gets creative pleasure from his collection of brightly colored rags. He sorts them over and over again, rejoicing in their hues and textures. He is never wearied of them. The parent learns to be grateful that pleasure finds its expression, if not in ways that benefit the world, at least in ways that satisfy and enrich the child. Quantitatively, of course, there is a difference between the bright rags and a box of paints that an artist uses. But qualitatively the two are the same to the boy and to the artist. Both find the same spiritual satisfaction.

To parents I say first that if you discover that your child cannot be normal, be glad if he is below the possibility of knowing his own condition. The burden of life has been removed from him and it rests only upon you, who can learn how to bear it.

To learn how to bear the inevitable sorrow is not easily done. I can look back on it now, the lesson learned, and see the steps; but when I was taking them they were hard indeed, each apparently insurmountable. For in addition to the practical problem of how to protect the child's life, which may last beyond the parent's, there is the problem of one's own self in misery. All the brightness of life is gone, all the pride in parenthood. There is more than pride gone, there is an actual sense of one's life being cut off in the child. The stream of the generations is stopped. Death would be far easier to bear, for death is final. What was is no more. How often did I cry out in my heart that it would be better if my child died! If that shocks you who have not known, it will not shock those who do know. I would have welcomed death for my child and would still welcome it, for then she would be finally safe.

It is inevitable that one ponders much on this matter of a kindly death. Every now and again I see in the newspapers the report of a man or woman who has put to death a mentally defective child. My heart goes out to such a one. I understand the love and despair which prompted the act. There is not only the despair that descends when the inevitable makes itself known, but there is the increasing despair of every day. For each day that makes clear that the child is only as he was yesterday drives the despair deeper, and there are besides the difficulties of care for such a child, the endless round of duties that seem to bear no fruit, tending a body that will be no more than a body however long it lives, gazing into the dull eyes that respond with no lively look, helping the fumbling hands—all these drive deeper the despair. And added to the despair is the terror and the question, "Who will do this in case I do not live?"

And yet I know that the parents of whom I read do wrong when they take to themselves a right which is not theirs and end the physical lives of their children. In love they may do it, and yet it is wrong. There is a sacred quality of life which none of us can fathom. All peoples feel it, for in all societies it is considered a sin for one human being to kill another for a reason of his own. Society decrees death for certain crimes, but the innocent may not be killed, and there is none more innocent than these children who never grow up. Murder remains murder. Were the right to kill a child put even into a parent's hands, the effect would be evil indeed in our world. Were the right to kill any innocent person assumed by society, the effect would be monstrous. For first it might be only the helpless children who were killed, but then it might seem right to kill the helpless old; and then the conscience would become so dulled that prejudice would give the right to kill, and persons of a certain color or creed might be destroyed. The only safety is to reject completely the possibility of death as a means of ending any innocent life, however useless. The damage is not to the one who is killed, but to the one who kills. Euthanasia is a long, smooth-sounding word, and it conceals its danger as long, smooth words do, but the danger is there, nevertheless.

It would be evasion, however, if I pretended that it was easy to accept the inevitable. For the sake of others who are walking that stony road, I will say that my inner rebellion lasted for many years. My common sense, my convictions of duty, all told me that I must not let the disaster spoil my own life or those of relatives and friends. But common sense and duty cannot always prevail when the heart is broken. My compromise was to learn how to act on the surface as much like my usual self as possible, to talk, to laugh, to seem to take an interest in what went on. Underneath the rebellion burned, and tears flowed the moment I was alone. This surface acting kept me, of course, from having any real contact with other people. Doubtless they felt the surface bright and shallow, and were perhaps repelled by something hard and cold beneath which they could not reach. Yet it was necessary to maintain the surface, for it was my own protection, too. It was not possible to share with anyone in those years my inner state.

I can speak with detachment of it now, for it is over. I have learned my lesson. But it is interesting to me and may be of some small importance to some, merely as a process, to speak of learning how to live with sorrow that cannot be removed. Let me speak of it so, then.

The first phase of this process was disastrous and disorganizing. As I said, there was no more joy left in anything. All human relationships became meaningless. Everything became meaningless. I took no more pleasure in the things I had enjoyed before; landscapes, flowers, music were empty. Indeed, I could not bear to hear music at all. It was years before I could listen to music. Even after the learning process had gone very far, and my spirit had become nearly reconciled through understanding, I could not hear music. I did my work during this time: I saw that my house was neat and clean, I cut flowers for the vases, I planned the gardens and tended my roses, and arranged for meals to be properly served. We had guests and I did my duty in the community. But none of it meant anything. My hands performed their routine. The hours when I really lived were when I was alone with my child. When I was safely alone I could let sorrow have its way, and in utter rebellion against fate my spirit spent its energy. Yet I tried to conceal my weeping from my child because she stared at me and laughed. It was this uncomprehending laughter which always and finally crushed my heart.

I do not know when the turn came, nor why. It came somehow out of myself. People were kind enough, but no help came from anyone. Perhaps that was my own fault. Perhaps I made my surface too smooth and natural so that no one could see beneath it. Partly that, perhaps, and partly it was, too, because people shrink from penetrating surfaces. Only those who know inescapable sorrow know what I mean.

It was in those days that I learned to distinguish between the two kinds of people in the world: those who have known inescapable sorrow and those who have not. For there are basically two kinds of sorrows: those which can be assuaged and those which cannot be. The death of parents is sad, for they cannot be replaced, but it is not inescapable sorrow. It is natural sorrow, that which one must expect in the normal course of life. The crippling of one's body, irremediably, is an inescapable sorrow. It has to be lived with; and more than that, it has to be used for some other sort of life than that planned in health. The sorrows which can be assuaged are those which life can cover and heal. Those which cannot be assuaged are those which change life itself and in a way themselves make life. Sorrows that can die can be assuaged, but living sorrow is never assuaged. It is a stone thrown into the stream, as Browning put it, and the water must divide itself and accommodate itself, for it cannot remove the stone.

I learned at last, merely by watching faces and by listening to voices, to know when I had found someone who knew what it was to live with sorrow that could not be ended. It was surprising and sad to discover how many such persons there were and to find how often the quality I discerned came from just such a sorrow as my own. It did not comfort me, for I could not rejoice in the knowledge that others had the same burden that I had, but it made me realize that others had learned how to live with it, and so could I. I suppose that was the beginning of the turn. For the despair into which I had sunk when I realized that nothing could be done for the child and that she would live on and on had become a morass into which I could easily have sunk into uselessness. Despair so profound and absorbing poisons the whole system and destroys thought and energy.

My own natural health, too, I suppose, had something to do with it. I saw that the sun rose and set, that the seasons came and went, that my garden bloomed and that upon the streets the people passed and laughter could be heard.

At any rate, the process of accommodation began. The first step was acceptance of what was. Perhaps it was consciously taken in a day. Perhaps there was a single moment in which I actually said to myself, "This thing is unchangeable, it will not leave me, no one can help me, I must accept it." But practically the step had to be taken many times. I slipped into the morass over and over again. The sight of a neighbor's normal little daughter talking and doing the things my child could never do was enough to send me down. But I learned not to stay down. I came up again and learned to say, "This is my life and I have to live it."

Having to live a life, it seemed rational as time went on to try to enjoy what I could in that life. Music was still too close to me, but there were other things I could enjoy—books, I remember, were first. Flowers, I think, came next. I began to care, mildly, about my roses. It all began, I remember, in a sort of wonder that such things went on as they had before, and then a realization that what had happened to me had actually changed nothing except myself.

Yet life did not really begin again until necessity drove me to think what I ought to do about the child's life. There were certain practical things that could and should be done. Was I to keep her with me, or should she find a home among children of her own kind? Would she be happier with me or with them? Had there been security in her life with me, I would have felt it best to keep her with me, for I did not believe that anyone could understand her as well as I did, or do for her what I could. Moreover, I had given her birth and she was my responsibility.

It was then that the solitary place in which she stood became apparent to me. The world is not shaped for the helpless. If I should die too young, what would become of her? We were living in China. The best that could be expected was that she would be taken to our country, the United States, and put into an institution. There, alone, she would have to make the adjustment of being without me and without her loving Chinese nurse and all that had meant home to her. She might not be able to make such an adjustment alone. Certainly she would not be able to understand why it had to be, and the puzzle and grief might disturb her beyond control. It came to me then that it would be best for her to make the adjustment while I lived, while I could help. She could gradually change her roots from this home to a new one, knowing that I was near and would come to see her again and again.

Upon this matter of her future security alone I made my decision. It was hastened, perhaps, by a situation peculiar to my life: that China was upset by civil wars and revolutions. I think my decision took its final shape on a certain day, of which I have written elsewhere, when a horde of communist soldiers forced Americans and other foreigners out of their homes, killed some of them and compelled the rest of us to hide for our lives. A kindly Chinese gave us the shelter of her little thatched hut, and there through that long day I faced death with all my family. But it was of my child that I thought most. If the moment of death came, I must contrive to have her killed first. I could not leave her in the hands of wild soldiers.

This situation, as I say, was peculiar, and of no moment to those for whom I write this story. But the essential question remains the same for all of us who have these children who never grow up. We have to think beyond our own lives for them.

It became apparent, too, as time went on, that my little daughter should find her own companions. The friends who came and went in my home could never be her friends. Kind and pitying as they were, they felt the child a strain upon them and they in turn were a strain upon her and upon me. It became clear indeed that I must seek and find her world and put her in it.

Again an incident, very slight in itself, crystallized my thinking. We had some American neighbors in our big

Chinese community, and one of the neighbors had a little girl just the age of mine. They had always gone to each other's parties. One day, however, the other little girl, having come over to play, was prattling as little girls will, and she said, "My mamma says don't have your poor little girl any more to my party, and so I can't ever have her next time."

Next time, indeed, the invitation did not come. The great separation had begun. I realized then that I must find another world for my child, one where she would not be despised and rejected, one where she could find her own level and have friends and affection, understanding and appreciation. I decided that day to find the right institution for her.

I might mention another circumstance peculiar to my situation. When I told one or two of my closest Chinese friends what I had decided upon, they were very much perturbed. Chinese do not believe in institutions. They feel that the helpless, young and old, should be cared for by the family, reasoning, and quite truly, that no stranger, however kind, can be trusted to be as kind as the family. There are no homes for the old in China, no orphanages except those started through western influence, no places for the insane or for the mentally defective. Such persons are cared for entirely at home, as long as they live. My Chinese friends therefore thought me very cruel to consider letting my child leave home. In vain I explained to them that the American family was not like theirs. The Chinese home is stable and it continues in the same house from generation to generation. All generations live under the same roof and are mutually responsible for and to one another. It is true that such a family home is ideal for the care of the helpless.

They could not believe that I had no such home even in my native land. My relatives were strange to me, since I had grown up far from them, and certainly they could not be expected to look after my helpless child were I to die. Moreover, they lived in separate homes of their own. They would consider it an imposition to have my child left in their care. Ours is an individualistic society, indeed, and the state must do for the individual what family does in the older civilizations. It was hard to explain this to my Chinese friends, and hard not to be moved by their appeals to me to keep the child with me.

The decision made, the next question was how it was to be done, and then when. I had found out enough to know that the sort of place I wanted my child to live in would cost money that I did not have. There was no one to pay for this except myself. I must myself devise means to do what I wanted to do for my child.

I am speaking now entirely about myself, and I realize that what I did cannot always be done. The fact is I had never considered money from the days when I first began to earn my own living, at least in part, when I was seventeen years old and in college. Independence had taught me that the important thing was to know what I wanted. Then I could always find means to get it. This habit of mine held. I decided that when the time came I would return to my country and search for the place which could become my child's home.

There is infinite relief in a decision. It provides a goal. A guiding rope was flung into the morass and I clung to it and dragged myself out of despair day by day, as the goal became more clear to me. Knowing what I was going to do and thinking how to do it did not heal the inescapable sorrow, but it helped me to live with it. I ceased to use all my spiritual energies in rebellion. I did not ask *why* so continually. The real secret of it was that I began to stop thinking of myself and my sorrow and began to think only of my child. This meant that I was not struggling against life, but slowly and sometimes blindly coming into accord with it. So long as I centered in myself, life was unbearable. When I shifted that center even a little, I began to understand that sorrow could be borne, not easily but possibly.

I felt, however, that before I let my child leave me I ought to try her abilities for myself and learn to know her thoroughly, so that I could make the best possible choice of her future home. For this I decided to take a year, during which all my time, aside from family essentials, would be spent with her. I would try to teach her to read, to write, to distinguish colors and, since she loved music, to learn notes and to sing little songs. Whether she could do this I did not know. It was as important for me to know if she could not as to know if she could.

In a curious way I was helped here by what was taking place in China. The rowdy capture of Nanking by the new revolutionary forces had compelled all white people to leave the city for a period. It was in early spring that the capture took place, and we went to Japan for a peaceful summer in the beautiful green mountains above the seaport of Nagasaki. It was a happy summer in its way. We lived in a small Japanese house in the woods, and bereft of possessions and responsibilities, it was a return to nature. For me, after the hard years, it was a time of healing. I knew no one except the friendly Japanese fisher-folk who came to sell crabs and fish at early morning. My child could run about as she liked, while I did my primitive housekeeping. I cooked on a charcoal brazier as the Japanese women did, and we lived upon rice and fish and fruit.

I shall pause here for a little gift of thanks to the Japanese people I met in those pleasant months of enforced holiday. Later in the summer I decided to take advantage of idleness and to make a journey through Japan. With my child I made that journey, traveling third class by day on the trains, both to save money and to meet the average Japanese people. We ate the little lunches we bought from venders at the station, small, clean, wooden boxes packed with compartments of rice, pickles and fish, and my child for the first time in her life had fresh pasteurized milk, hot and in sealed bottles.

At night we left the train and slept in clean little village inns where we saw only Japanese faces. We left our shoes at the doorway, and deft Japanese maids put slippers on our feet and led us to a hot bath and then to our room. Then the evening meal was served in lacquered wooden bowls, a chicken or beef broth, eggs, fish, rice and tea. Afterward the spotless soft quilts were brought from the wall closets, and spread on the clean matting floor for us. I woke often in the night to gaze into a dim moonlit garden, perhaps only a few feet square, which somehow suggested, nevertheless, space and infinity. It is the Japanese genius. Everywhere we met with kindness and courtesy. There was no sign that anyone saw my child as strange. She was accepted for what she was and most tenderly treated. That brought healing too.

In the late autumn, before Christmas, we went back to China to live for a year in Shanghai. It was still not safe, we were told, to return to Nanking. That year alone with my child was a profound education for me. As I look back on it, I see that it was the beginning of whatever real knowledge I have of the human mind. We had three rooms at the top of a house shared with two other families, refugees like ourselves. There I planned my child's days and my own, so much time each day devoted to finding out what she could learn. I willed myself to patience and submission to her capacities. Impatience was a sin. So the long year began, work interspersed with exercise and play.

The detail of those months is unimportant now, but I will simply say that I found that the child could learn to read simple sentences, that she was able, with much effort, to write her name, and that she loved songs and was able to sing simple ones. What she was able to achieve was of no significance in itself. I think she might have been able to proceed further, but one day, when, pressing her always very gently but still steadily and perhaps in my anxiety rather relentlessly, I happened to take her little right hand to guide it in writing a word. It was wet with perspiration. I took both her hands and opened them and saw they were wet. I realized then that the child was under intense strain, that she was trying her very best for my sake, submitting to something she did not in the least understand, with an angelic wish to please me. She was not really learning anything.

It seemed my heart broke all over again. When I could control myself I got up and put away the books forever. Of what use was it to push this mind beyond where it could function? She might after much effort be able to read a little, but she could never enjoy books. She might learn to write her name, but she would never find in writing a means of communication. Music she could hear with joy, but she could not make it. Yet the child was human. She had a right to happiness, and her happiness was to be able to live where she could function.

"Let's go outside and play with the kitties," I said.

Her little face took on a look of incredulous joy, and that was my reward.

Happiness, I now determined, was to be her atmosphere. I gave up all ambition for her, all pride, and accepted her exactly as she was, expecting nothing, grateful if some flash came through the dimness of her mind. Wherever she could be most happy would be her home. I kept her with me until she was nine years old, and then I set out in search of her final home.

III

I came to my own country as a stranger. There was disadvantage in this, for I had no friends to guide me, nor any who knew in any way what I needed or how to help me. Yet there was advantage too. I knew what I wanted to find and I had learned from my life among the Chinese to look for essentials—that is, for human quality. I had determined that I would not judge by money alone. If the right place cost a great deal, I would find some way to pay for it. I was young, I was strong, I was well educated. With those three gifts, I could provide somehow for the child.

I learned a great deal in the next year. It took me in many directions indeed. I had a long list of schools and institutions and I asked for others as I went. Of that intensive search it would be useless to tell every detail, but for those who must make a similar search it may be useful to know certain things.

First of all, I learned not to judge an institution by its grounds and equipment. Some of the finest and most expensively equipped schools were the worst, so far as the children were concerned. I remember one such place. I had spent a whole day with the headmistress. She showed me every detail of the splendidly planned grounds and houses. The children were well fed and well cared for, obviously. She had a resident doctor and a resident psychologist. The attendants for the children were neat and pleasant. There were an excellent school building and a good exhibit of handicraft, done by the children. There was a department of music. Every effort, she assured me, was made to develop the children to the height of their potentiality. She herself was competent, brisk, not unkind. I tried to think of my little girl beside her and could not quite imagine warmth between them, but of course the headmistress would not have much to do with any individual child. So well impressed was I as the day went on that I was beginning to think of the fabulous annual fee and to plan how it could be found. Evening came, and I sat on the wide porch, still with the headmistress, waiting for the bus that was to take me away. Then something happened which undid all the day.

A car stopped and a group of young girls in their teens, all children in the school, mounted the steps and crossed the porch. They greeted the headmistress very properly and she returned their greeting. I saw her watching them sharply.

Suddenly she called to them, "Girls, stop!"

They stopped, half frightened.

The headmistress said in her clear, peremptory way, "How often have I told you to hold up your heads? Go back to the steps and walk across the porch again!"

They obeyed instantly while she watched.

When they had gone into the house she turned to me with a complacent explanatory air. "It is part of my work to teach the girls how to enter a room properly and how to leave it. Feeble-minded people always walk with their heads hanging—it's characteristic. I have to break them of it."

"Why?" I asked.

She shrugged her shoulders. "These girls all come of good families, people in society," she explained. "The parents don't want to be ashamed of taking them about." She laughed half contemptuously. "Why, I even have to teach them how to hold a hand at bridge and look as though they were playing!"

"Why do you do it?" I asked.

"I have to make my living," she said honestly enough.

We parted on that, but I knew that I would never send my child to her handsome institution. I wanted to find a man or woman who thought of the children first. Of course we must all live, but it is amazing how easy it is to find bread when one does not put it first.

That experience taught me thereafter to look for the right person at the head of the institution. I knew that the employees would be no better than the head, therefore the head must be the best. I ceased to look at equipment and housing. There must of course be space for play, and ample sunshine and fresh air. I rejected the extreme north country because the season outside was so short. My child had been used to a semi-tropical air and much outdoor play. But beyond space and a minimum of cleanliness and care, I began to look for the right people, people who were warm and human.

I might say here that since I was not resident in my own country I belonged to no state and therefore state institutions were not easily open to me. Moreover, they had long waiting lists, and though I visited them, most of them were overcrowded and the children lived in strict routine. Oh, how my heart suffered for those big rooms of children sitting dully on benches, waiting, waiting!

"What are they waiting for?" I asked my guide one day.

"They aren't waiting for anything," he replied in surprise. "They're just sitting. That's all they want to do."

"How do you know they wouldn't like to do something more?" I asked.

He evaded the question. "We get them all up a couple of times a day and make them walk around the building."

But I know the children were really waiting. They were waiting for something pleasant to happen to them. Perhaps they did not know they were waiting, but they were. I know

now that there is no mind so dim that it does not feel pain and pleasure. These, too, were human beings—that, I perceived, was the important thing to understand, and many of those who cared for them did not understand it. The children who never grow are human beings and they suffer as human beings, inarticulately but deeply nevertheless. The human creature is always more than an animal.

That is the one thing we must never forget. He is forever more than a beast. Though the mind has gone away, though he cannot speak or communicate with anyone, the human stuff is there, and he belongs to the human family.

I saw this wonderfully exemplified in one state institution. When I first visited the place it was an abode of horror. The children, some young in body, some old, were apparently without any minds whatever. The average mental age was estimated at less than one year. They were herded together like dogs. They wore baglike garments of rough calico or burlap. Their food was given to them on the floor and they snatched it up. No effort was made to teach them toilet habits. The floors were of cement and were hosed two or three times a day. The beds were pallets on the floor, and filthy. There were explanations, of course. I was told that these children could be taught nothing, that they merely existed until they died. Worst of all to me was that there was not one thing of beauty anywhere, nothing for the children to look at, no reason for them to lift their heads or put out their hands.

Some years later I went back again. I had heard there was a new man in charge, a young man who was different. I found that he was different, and because he was, he had made the whole institution different. It was as crowded as ever, but wholly changed. It was like a home. There were gay curtains at the windows and bright linoleums on the floors. In the various rooms the children had been segregated, babies were with babies, and older children with their own kind. There were chairs and benches and the children sat on them. There were flowers in the windows and toys on the floor. The children were decent and even wore pretty clothes, and they were all clean. The old sickening smell was gone. There was a dining room, and there were tables, on which were dishes and spoons and mugs.

"Are the children now of a higher grade?" I asked the young man.

"No," he said, smiling, "many of them are the same children."

"But I was told they could not be taught."

"They can all be taught something," he replied. "When they can't manage alone, someone helps them."

Then he showed me the things they had made, actually little baskets and mats, simple and full of mistakes, but to me wonderful. And the children who had made them were so proud of what they had done. They came up to us, and though they could not speak, they knew what they had done.

"Has their mental age gone up?" I asked.

"A little, on the average," he replied. "But it isn't only mental age that counts with them—or with anybody, for that matter."

"How did you do it?" I asked.

"I treat them as human beings," he said simply.

When my search ended it was at another place where I found such a person. Without looking at the buildings or the grounds, I knew when I entered the office and shook hands with the quiet, gray-haired man who greeted me with a gentle voice that I had found what I wanted. Of course I did not decide upon impulse, I told him about my child and what it was that I looked for, and he listened. There was something in the way he listened. He was sympathetic, but not with effort. He was not eager. He said diffidently that he did not know whether I would be satisfied with his school, but we might look around. So we did look around, and what I saw was that every child's face lit when he came into the cottages, and that there was a clamor of voices to greet him and call his name—Uncle Ed, they called him. I saw that he took time to play with them and that he let them hug his knees and look in his pockets where there were small chocolates—very tiny ones, not enough to spoil a child's appetite. He knew every child and his seeing eyes were noticing everything every-where. He greeted the attendants with courtesy and when he made a suggestion—that Jimmy, for instance, should have a lower chair upon which to sit, and so the legs of the chair he liked best could be cut off to suit—the attendant was quick to agree.

The buildings were pleasant and adequate, but not nearly so handsome as some I had seen. The atmosphere was what I felt. It was warm and free and friendly. I saw children playing around the yards behind the cottages, making mud pies and behaving as though they were at home. I saw a certain motto repeated again and again on the walls, on the stationery, hanging above the head's own desk. It was this: "Happiness first and all else follows."

The head smiled when he saw my eyes resting on the words. "That's not just sentimentality," he said. "It is the fruit of experience. We've found that we cannot teach a child anything unless his mind and heart are free of unhappiness. The only child who can learn is the happy child."

I knew enough about teaching to know that this is a sound principle in any education. It was comforting and reassuring to find it the cornerstone here upon which all else was built. I said to myself that I would look no more.

Upon a September day I brought my little girl to the place I had found. We walked about to accustom her to the new playgrounds and I went with her to the corner where her bed stood. I met the woman who was to be her attendant, as well as the superintendent of girls. The child clung to my hand and I to hers. What went on in her little mind I do not know, but I think some foreboding was there. We had never been separated, and the time was coming when there must be a separation almost as final as death. I would come back to see her often, and she could come sometimes to see me, but the separation was there, nevertheless. We were to be parted. Even though I believed that it was best for her safety that she find her permanent shelter here, the fact that she would need lifelong shelter was the primary cruelty.

In the afternoon of that day which was so dreadful in its passing the head asked me to come to the assembly hall. The children were all to gather there for some music. In his kindness he asked me to sit on the platform with him and to speak to the children for a few minutes about Chinese children. Some of them, he said, would understand.

There are moments which crystallize within an instant the meaning of years. Such a one came to me when I stood on the platform of that room and saw before me hundreds of children's faces looking up at me. What heartache loomed behind each one, what years of pain, what tears, what frightful disappointment and despair! They were here for life, prisoners of their fate. And among them, one of them, my child must henceforth be.

The kind man at whose side I stood must have discerned something of what I felt, for when he saw I could not speak he told a little story and made the children laugh and I was able to go on again. I think I never tried more earnestly to

interest an audience, never had I put myself so wholeheart-
edly into any effort as I did into that half hour of talk with
those children. I could not say what was in my heart. I could
not tell them that I understood their lives better than I understood anything else, because I had lived through such a life.
I had to tell small childish things that they could grasp, and
my reward was their fresh laughter. After it was over, the head
took me aside alone and talked to me gently and gravely. I
have never forgotten his words. "You must remember," he
said, "that these are happy children. They are safe here. They
will never know distress or want. They will never know struggle or defeat, nor will sorrow ever touch them. No demands
are made upon them which they cannot meet. The joys which
they can appreciate they have. Your child will escape all suffering. Will you remember that and let it be a comfort to you?
Remember that there is a sorrow worse than one's own—it
is to see a beloved person suffer without being able to help.
That sorrow you will never have."

Many a time since then when I have thought of the child
and the waters have seemed to close over my head, I have
remembered those kind and wise words. As long as the child
is happy, am I not strong enough to bear what is to be borne?

I left her there and, following the request of the school,
I did not visit her for a month. The head believed that a full
month was needed for the new roots to be put down, and to
see the parents delayed the necessary process. They would

tell me, he promised, if anything went wrong. So I tore myself away, leaving her for the first time in our lives.

Of that month I need not speak. Any parent like me will know the doubts that beset me. To leave a child who cannot write a letter, who cannot even make known in words what she feels and needs, seemed to me at times the height of cruelty. These times came in the night, and only the thought of a future with the child grown old and me gone could keep me from hurrying to the nearest railway station. Ah, well, there are many who know such hours in the night!

It would be pleasant to say that when I went back to the school at the end of the month I found the child happy and well. This was not true. Her distraught little face, her pitiful joy at seeing me brought back all the doubts again and I was ready to pack her trunk and bring her home.

The elderly matron stood looking at us. "She has been quite naughty," she said gravely. "She has not wanted to do what the other children do and she has cried a great deal. We have had to deal with her."

"Deal with her?" I asked.

"Yes. When she ran out of the house we had to restrain her."

"She is used to freedom," I murmured. "And of course she was running out to look for me."

"She cannot run outside alone," the matron said, "and she must learn to obey. When she learns, she will be happy as the others are."

Protest was thick in my throat, but I choked it back. "I will take her out for a little walk," I said.

As soon as we were outside and alone she was as happy as a songbird again, but she clutched my hand as though she would never let it go. I went in search of the head. He was there in his office and he welcomed me and spoke to the child. She seemed to know him and not be afraid of him, and this meant he had been to see her himself.

I began at once. "I think I cannot leave her here," I told him. "The matron says that they have had to restrain her, whatever that means. But surely they understand that a little child like this cannot suddenly be happy without the home she has always had. She has never been among strangers. She cannot understand why her life is completely and suddenly changed. Do the children have to be forced into a routine? Must they walk in line into the dining room, for example?"

This and much more I said. He let me say it all while his eyes were kind upon us.

"It is not possible for your child to live here exactly as she has in your house," he said when I had finished. "Here she is one of many. She will be individually cared for and watched and taught, it is true, but she cannot behave as though she were the only child. This will mean some loss of freedom to her. This loss you must weigh against the gain. She is safe here. She has companionship. When she learns to fall in with the others in the small routines that are necessary in any big family, she will even enjoy the sense of being with the crowd. She has to learn, you know. But rest assured that she will be taught only those things which she is able to learn and nothing will be forced on her that is beyond her.

"Try to think of what she will be a year from now, five years from now. Try to consider justly whether this place is the right one for her home. Don't lose a larger value in some small present dissatisfaction."

I said, "It is so hard because she doesn't understand why it is all necessary or that it is for her good."

"None of us really understands why," he said in his same gentle voice. "You do not understand why you have had to have the child like this at all. You cannot see that there is any good in it anywhere."

I could not indeed.

"You cannot shield your child from everything," he went on. "She is a human creature and she must bear her little share, too, of what is common to all human life."

Much else he said and I sat listening and the child sat content by my side. When he finished I knew that he had done what he meant to do—he had helped me to find strength to think of the child's larger good.

I stayed with her for only a day, because they said it would be better not to stay too long the first time. Then I went away. I shall never forget as long as I live that I had to pull her little arms away from around my neck and that I dared not look back. I knew the matron was holding her fast and I knew I must not see it, lest my courage fail.

Years have passed since that day. I came to live in America, not far from her, and I visit her often. She is used now to my coming and going, and yet even now there is the brief clinging when I leave. "I want to go home," she whispers again and again. She comes home sometimes, too, and is filled with joy for a few days. But here is the comfort I take nowadays. After she has been at home a week or so, she begins to miss the other home. She inquires after "the girls," she asks for some toy or musical instrument or record that she left behind. At last almost willingly she goes back again, after making sure that I am coming soon to see her. The long struggle is over. The adjustment has been made. When the wakeful hours come in the night I comfort myself, thinking that if I should die before I wake, as the old childish prayer has it, her life would go on just the same. Much of the money that I have been able to earn has gone into making this security for her. I have a sense of pride that she will be dependent on no one as long as she lives, and whether or not I live. I have done all that could be done.

I realize that many parents cannot be so fortunate as I have been in being able to make a child secure. Some of them have come to me with children like mine and have asked me what to do. They have told me that they have little money or that they have other children and what there is must be divided. The helpless child cannot have everything, however the parents' hearts are torn. They are right, of course. Speaking coldly, if it is possible to do so, the normal children are more useful to society perhaps than the helpless ones.

And yet I wonder if that is so. My helpless child has taught me so much. She has taught me patience, above all else. I come of a family impatient with stupidity and slowness, and I absorbed the family intolerance of minds less quick than our own. Then there was put into my sole keeping this pitiful mind, struggling against I know not what handicap. Could I despise it for what was no fault of its own? That indeed would have been the most cruel injustice. While I tried to find out its slight abilities I was compelled both by love and justice to learn tender and careful patience. It was not always easy. Natural impatience burst forth time and again, to my shame, and it seemed useless to try to teach. But justice reasoned with me thus: "This mind has the right to its fullest development too. It may be very little, but the right is the same as yours, or any other's. If you refuse it the right to know, in so far as it can know, you do a wrong."

So by this most sorrowful way I was compelled to tread, I learned respect and reverence for every human mind. It was my child who taught me to understand so clearly that all people are equal in their humanity and that all have the same human rights. None is to be considered less, as a human being, than any other, and each must be given his place and his safety in the world. I might never have learned this in any other way. I might have gone on in the arrogance of my own intolerance for those less able than myself. My child taught me humility.

My child taught me to know, too, that mind is not all of the human creature. Though she cannot speak to me clearly, there are other ways in which she communicates. She has an extraordinary integrity of character. She seems to sense deception and she will not tolerate it. She is a child of great purity. She will not tolerate habits that are filthy and her sense of dignity is complete. No one may take liberties with her person. Neither will she endure cruelty. If a child in her cottage screams she hurries to see why, and if the child is being struck by another child or if an attendant is too harsh, she cries aloud and goes in search of the housemother. She has been known to push away the offending one. She will not endure injustice. An attendant, laughing, said to me one day, "We have to treat her fairly or she makes more trouble for us."

What I am trying to say is that there is a whole personality not concerned with the mind, and children mentally deficient often compensate for their lack by other qualities of goodness.

This is a very important fact and it has been so recognized. Psychologists working with mentally retarded children at The Training School in Vineland, New Jersey, have found that while the I. Q. may be very low indeed a child actually may function a good deal higher because of his social sense, his feeling of how he ought to behave, his pride, his kindness, his wish to be liked. Acting upon this observation, they developed the Social Maturity Scale, to complement the Binet Scale earlier brought from France and adapted for use in the United States. What is true of the retarded child is also true of the normal one. A high intelligence may be a curse to society, as it has often been, unless it is accompanied by qualities of character which provide social maturity, and the less brilliant child who has these qualities is a better citizen and often achieves more individually than the high intelligence without them.

Today this Vineland Social Maturity Scale is very widely used in the armed forces, in schools and colleges, in aptitude tests, wherever normal individuals are measured. We have to thank the helpless children for teaching us that mere intelligence is not enough.

They have taught us much more. They have taught us how people learn. The minds of retarded children are sane minds, normal except that, being arrested, the processes are slowed. But they learn in the same ways that the normal minds do, repeated many more times. Psychologists, observing the slower processes, have been able to discover, exactly as though in a slow-motion picture, the way the human creature acquires new knowledge and new habits. Our educational techniques for normal children have been vastly improved by what the retarded children have taught us.

In the years which have passed since I led my child into her own world, again and again I have been able to find comfort in the fact that her life, with others, has been of use in enlarging the whole body of our knowledge. When one has learned how to live with inescapable sorrow, one learns, too, how to find comfort by the way.

When I speak of comfort I think now of other parents than myself. I think of those who bring me their children and ask what to do for them. Almost the first question they ask is, "Are private schools and institutions so much better than the state ones that we ought to make all the family sacrifice to the utmost for the sake of one?"

My answer is this: A good private school is usually better than the average state institution. There is less crowding and more individual attention. But even this depends somewhat upon the state. There are states where the institutions are remarkably good, the employees well paid, a pension system established and every inducement offered for good people to stay. There are other states where the institutions are medieval. Parents must examine their own state institutions. Where there are ample family funds, a good private institution has advantages. Yet the weakness in most private institutions is that often they do not continue beyond the lifetime of the person who establishes them. Some of the finest and most elaborate private institutions will close when the head dies, and the children then must be scattered and must make their adjustments all over again. It is essential in choosing your child's home that you find an institution which is not dependent upon any one man, but which is controlled by a self-perpetuating board of trustees and has endowments to carry it through the hard years. The state institutions have, of course, an immense advantage in that they are permanent, and once a child enters he is secure for life.

I answer the parents by saying that where a private institution would bring severe sacrifice on every member of the family for the sake of one, I would find a good state institution, even if I had to move my home to another state, and there I would put my child.

When the child is safely in his new home, what are the further responsibilities of the parent? They are many. The child needs the parents as much as before. There should be regular visits, as frequent as possible. Do not think that the children do not know. I have to endure heartbreaking moments every time I go to visit my child, for inevitably some other little child comes and takes my hand and leans against me and asks, "Where is my mamma?"

The housemother whispers over her head, "Poor little thing, her folks never come to see her. Her grandmother came to see her two years ago and that's the last."

The little thing's heart is slowly breaking. For these children are always children. They are loving and affectionate and they crave to be loved exactly as all children do. There are other children who come to tell me, eyes glowing, "My daddy and mummy came last week to see me!" Even the ones who cannot speak will come to show me a new doll that the parents brought.

Ah, they know, because they feel! The mind seems to have very little to do with the capacity to feel.

Another responsibility of the parent is to watch always the person in direct charge of the child. I said that I chose my child's permanent home by finding as the head the sort of person whom I could trust. Today, were I to choose again, I would also go into every cottage and look at the type of attendant there. Were they the hard-faced professional type, the ones who go from institution to institution, callous, cruel, ready to strike a child who does not conform, I would reject that place. For the most important person in an institution, so far as the child is concerned, and therefore so far as the parent is concerned, is not the executive, and not the man or woman in the offices, not even the doctor and the psychologist and the teacher, but the attendant, the person who has the direct care of the child.

A cruel and selfish attendant who has not at heart the welfare of the child can undo all the work of the teacher and the psychologist. Your child cannot benefit by any teaching unless he is happy in his daily life in his cottage. The attendant must be a person of affectionate and invincibly kind nature, child loving, able to discipline without physical force, in control because the children love him or her. Whether this attendant is well educated is not important. He must understand children, for he has in his care perpetual children.

Any sign of cruelty or injustice or carelessness on the part of attendants should be at once reported by conscientious parents. Do not think that secret bribes or tips will protect your child from a bad attendant. He will take your money and when he is alone with the children, as he is so much of the time, he will treat your child exactly as he does the others.

A third responsibility which the parent has to the child in the institution is to see that the atmosphere in which he lives is one of hopefulness. I have observed that this atmosphere is best in those institutions which carry on research as one of their functions. A place where the care is merely custodial is apt to degenerate into something routine and dead. No child ought to be merely something to be cared for and preserved from harm. His life, however simple, means something. He has something to contribute, even though he is helpless. There are reasons for his condition, causes which may be discovered. If he himself cannot be cured or even changed, others may be born whole because of what he has been able to teach, all unknowingly.

The Training School at Vineland is an excellent example of what I mean. For many years it has maintained an active research department. As I said, it was the first institution in this country to use and adapt the Binet test, and there the Social Maturity Scale was developed. Its work with birth-injured children and cerebral palsy has been notable, and the vigorous men and women who have spent their lives there learning from the children, in order that they may know better how to prevent and to cure, have infused vitality into the life of the institution, and into the whole subject of mental deficiency beyond.

Parents may find comfort, I say, in knowing that their children are not useless, but that their lives, limited as they are, are of great potential value to the human race. We learn as much from sorrow as from joy, as much from illness as from health, from handicap as from advantage—and indeed perhaps more. Not out of fullness has the human soul always reached its highest, but often out of deprivation. This is not to say that sorrow is better than happiness, illness than health, poverty than richness. Had I been given the choice, I would a thousand times over have chosen to have my child sound and whole, a normal woman today, living a woman's life. I miss eternally the person she cannot be. I am not resigned and never will be. Resignation is something still and dead, an inactive acceptance that bears no fruit. On the contrary, I rebel against the unknown fate that fell upon her somewhere and stopped her growth. Such things ought not to be, and because it has happened to me and because I know what this sorrow is I devote myself and my child to the work of doing all we can to prevent such suffering for others.

There is one little boy in my child's school whom I often go to see. He is little because he is only about seven in his mind. His body now is almost forty years old. He has a grave face and there is a forlorn look in his eyes. His father is a famous man, wealthy and well known. But he never comes to see his son. The boy's mother is dead. When someone approached this father for a gift for a new kind of research he banged his desk with his fist and said, "I will not give one cent! All my money is going to normal people."

Callous? He is not callous. His heart is bleeding, his pride is broken. His son is an imbecile—*his* son! In these years he has thought of himself and his loss, and he has missed the joy he might have had in his child—not the joy he sought, of course, but joy for all that.

There is another father—they are not always fathers, either—whose boy loves to work with the cows. I see the lad sometimes, a handsome fellow. He is usually in the dairy barn, caring for the cows, brushing them clean, loving them. I saw his father there one day, that brilliant able man, and he said, "It does seem that if my boy can learn to use the milking machine he could learn to do something better."

The head happened to be there that day and he said, "But there is nothing better for him, don't you see? The best thing in the world for each of us is that which we can best do, because it gives us the feeling of being useful. That's happiness."

So what I would say to parents is something I have learned through the years and it took me long to learn it, and I am still learning. When your little child is born to you not whole and sound as you had hoped, but warped and defective in body or mind or perhaps both, remember this is still your child. Remember, too, that the child has his right to life, whatever that life may be, and he has the right to happiness, which you must find for him. Be proud of your child, accept him as he is and do not heed the words and stares of those who know no better. This child has a meaning for you and for all children. You will find a joy you cannot now suspect in fulfilling his life for and with him. Lift up your head and go your appointed way.

I speak as one who knows.

Yet none of us lives in the past, if we are still alive ourselves. It is inevitable that, as young parents in their time experience again the old agony and despair when their children are among those who can never grow, they demand some cause for hope. Other ills have been cured and research is being carried on for those we still do not know how to heal. All must be healed, of course. People must not die of cancer or polio or heart disease. Neither should they be mentally deficient if it can be prevented or cured. There cannot be a choice of which will be first. The battle of life must be fought on all fronts at the same time.

Therefore, I say, we must also fight for the right of our children to be born sound and whole. There must not be children who cannot grow. Year by year their number must be decreased until preventable causes of mental deficiency are prevented. The need is more pressing than the public knows. Our state institutions are dangerously overcrowded and unless research is hastened, millions of dollars must go into more institutions. Even if boarding homes are multiplied, the care of these children must be paid for, in the vast majority of cases, by public funds. How much wiser and more hopeful it would be to pay for scientific research which would make such care unnecessary! Let us remember that more than half of the mentally deficient in this country are so from noninherited causes, and these causes can be prevented, did we know what they are.

Present care, moreover, is very inadequate. State institutions are able to provide very little of the education that might release a good many of the children to normal, if protected, life. It is not possible to do much educating with an overworked staff in an overcrowded institution. In some states the higher positions in these institutions are still political plums, and the lives of the children are at the mercy of a succession of ignorant men. Private institutions, if they are good ones, are too expensive for the average family.

Yet I believe that the private institution has an indispensable place in our American system. Our notable scientific advance has been the result of private persons working in privately owned places. Public funds have developed very little scientific knowledge except for military purposes. So now I believe that research into this most necessary field, the study of the causes and cure of mental deficiency, must, in accordance with American tradition, take place in small private institutions where scientists can work in freedom. Such research should be co-ordinated so there will be no time wasted in duplication.

Something, of course, has already been done. I have spoken of the notable work of the Research Department at The Training School in Vineland, New Jersey. We know that at least 50 per cent of the mentally deficient children now in the United States can be educated to be productive members of society. *Education* alone would relieve our overcrowded public institutions. Studies have shown that there are nineteen types of jobs that can be done by an adult whose mentality is no more than that of a six-year-old child. Twenty per cent of all work in the United States is done by the unskilled worker.

We know, too, some of the reasons for injury to the brain, both prenatal and postnatal, but we do not know enough. A little physical remedial work is being done for the injured brains which are the chief causes of mental deficiency, but it is still experimental and confined largely to the limited though important field of cerebral palsy, where the decreased blood supply to the brain is the apparent cause for mental deficiency. Results are still too new to be relied upon, but in one institution they were reported as hopeful. 34 per cent of those operated upon showed definite mental improvement, an additional 51 per cent showed changes for the better in alertness, muscular control, interest span, appetite and increased irritability.

I speak of all this merely as grounds for hope, if and when research really begins in the causes and cure for mental deficiency on a scale comparable to that now being done in other fields. Hope is essential for activity.

Those who have children who can never grow—and few are the families who have not one somewhere—must and will work with renewed effort when they realize that more than half the children now mentally deficient need not have been so. They must and will work still harder when they realize that more than half now mentally deficient can, with proper education and environment, live and work in normal society, instead of being idle in inadequate institutions.

Hope brings comfort. What has been need not forever continue to be so. It is too late for some of our children, but if their plight can make people realize how unnecessary much of the tragedy is, their lives, thwarted as they are, will not have been meaningless.

Again, I speak as one who knows.

ABOUT THE AUTHOR

Pearl S. Buck (1892–1973) was a bestselling and Nobel Prize–winning author. Her classic novel *The Good Earth* (1931) was awarded a Pulitzer Prize and William Dean Howells Medal. Born in Hillsboro, West Virginia, Buck was the daughter of missionaries and spent much of the first half of her life in China, where many of her books are set. In 1934, civil unrest in China forced Buck back to the United States. Throughout her life she worked in support of civil and women's rights, and established Welcome House, the first international, interracial adoption agency. In addition to her highly acclaimed novels, Buck wrote two memoirs and biographies of both of her parents. For her body of work, Buck received the Nobel Prize for Literature in 1938, the first American woman to have done so. She died in Vermont.

PEARL S. BUCK

FROM OPEN ROAD MEDIA

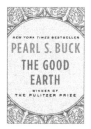  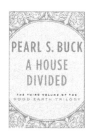

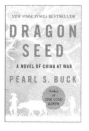 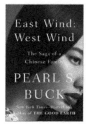 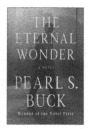 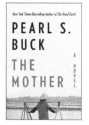

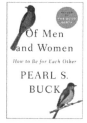 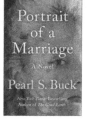 

OPEN ROAD

INTEGRATED MEDIA

CPSIA information can be obtained
at www.ICGtesting.com
Printed in the USA
BVHW081526130119
537723BV00002B/139/P